AEROPLANES
ROCKETS & BALLOONS

CHRISTOPHER RAWSON
ILLUSTRATED BY
STEPHEN CARTWRIGHT
CONSULTANT EDITOR
BILL GUNSTON

TIGER BOOKS INTERNATIONAL

 Stephen Cartwright's duck is on every double-page picture in this book. Can you find it?

Getting off the ground

For hundreds of years people wanted to fly. No one knew how to do it but they kept on trying.

In 1487 Leonardo da Vinci drew a flying machine. People laughed and said it would never work.

1 John Damian

In 1507 John Damian set out to fly from Scotland to France with wings he had made with feathers.

2

He jumped off a high tower. But the wings did not keep him up and he landed in the middle of a dung heap.

1 Sir George Cayley

Sir George Cayley built the first glider which took off and flew through the air in 1853.

2

It was pulled down a slope until it lifted off the ground. It flew across a valley, piloted by his coachman.

3

But when he landed, the coachman was so frightened, he refused to work for Sir George ever again.

Pedal power

Some people thought they would be able to fly if they fixed wings to their bicycles.

But it was impossible for them to pedal fast enough and they never managed to get off the ground.

Clement Ader

This Frenchman made a plane like a bat. It had a steam engine but did not really fly properly.

Otto Lilienthal

This famous German pilot made and flew the first hang glider in 1891.

He ran down a specially-made hill, carrying his glider until he took off.

Jean Marie le Bris

Another Frenchman tried to take off by tying his aeroplane to a cart.

The ropes were cut as the cart ran downhill. But the plane still would not fly.

Felix du Temple

FLYING MACHINE

WOODEN RAMP

The first aeroplane to take off with an engine looked like this.

It ran down a sloping ramp to get up speed and flew off the end.

But the steam engine which turned the propeller was too heavy.

After only a few metres in the air, the plane dived into the ground.

3

Early Flyers

1 The Wright Brothers

Two bicycle makers in America, called Wilbur and Orville Wright, had always longed to fly.

They studied other people's drawings and plans of aeroplanes, and watched how birds flew.

Their first flying machine had no engine. It would lift off the ground in a strong wind.

Sometimes they crashed but tried again and learned how to control a flying machine.

The Rheims Airshow

The first big airshow was held in a farmer's field near Rheims in France, in 1909. Out of 38 planes, only 23 took off. There were lots of competitions to find out which plane could fly the highest, the fastest, the furthest without stopping, and could carry the most passengers.

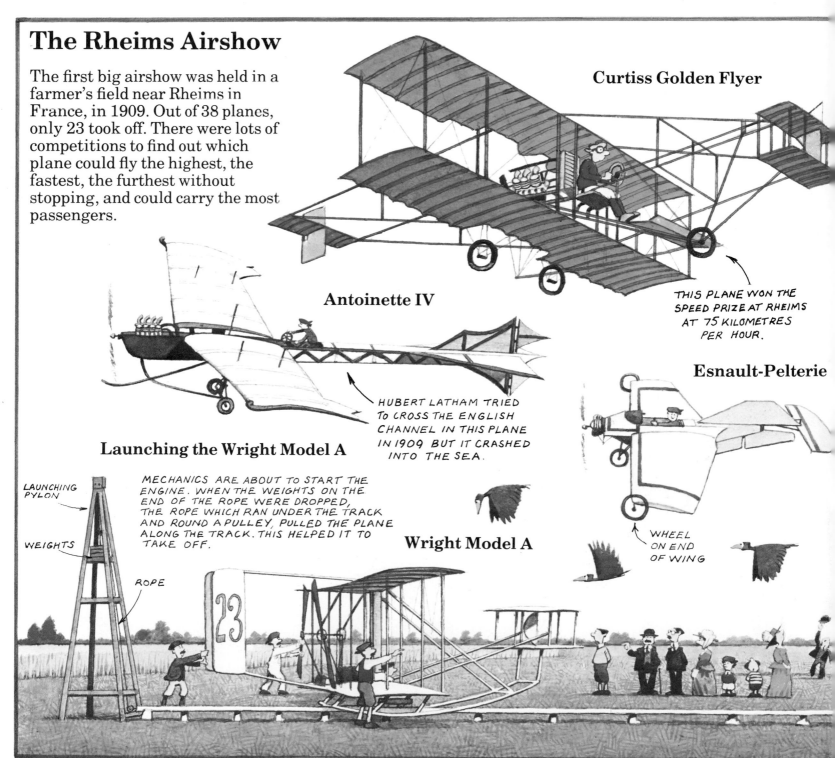

Curtiss Golden Flyer

THIS PLANE WON THE SPEED PRIZE AT RHEIMS AT 75 KILOMETRES PER HOUR.

Antoinette IV

HUBERT LATHAM TRIED TO CROSS THE ENGLISH CHANNEL IN THIS PLANE IN 1909 BUT IT CRASHED INTO THE SEA.

Esnault-Pelterie

WHEEL ON END OF WING

Launching the Wright Model A

LAUNCHING PYLON

WEIGHTS

ROPE

MECHANICS ARE ABOUT TO START THE ENGINE. WHEN THE WEIGHTS ON THE END OF THE ROPE WERE DROPPED, THE ROPE WHICH RAN UNDER THE TRACK AND ROUND A PULLEY, PULLED THE PLANE ALONG THE TRACK. THIS HELPED IT TO TAKE OFF.

Wright Model A

4

Then they built a special aeroplane engine with two propellers for their next aeroplane.

5

They tossed a coin to decide who would be the first to fly it. Wilbur won – but he crashed.

6

Two days later, when the plane was mended, it was Orville's turn to try. He was successful.

The Wrights' plane took off and made three successful flights. It was 17 December, 1903.

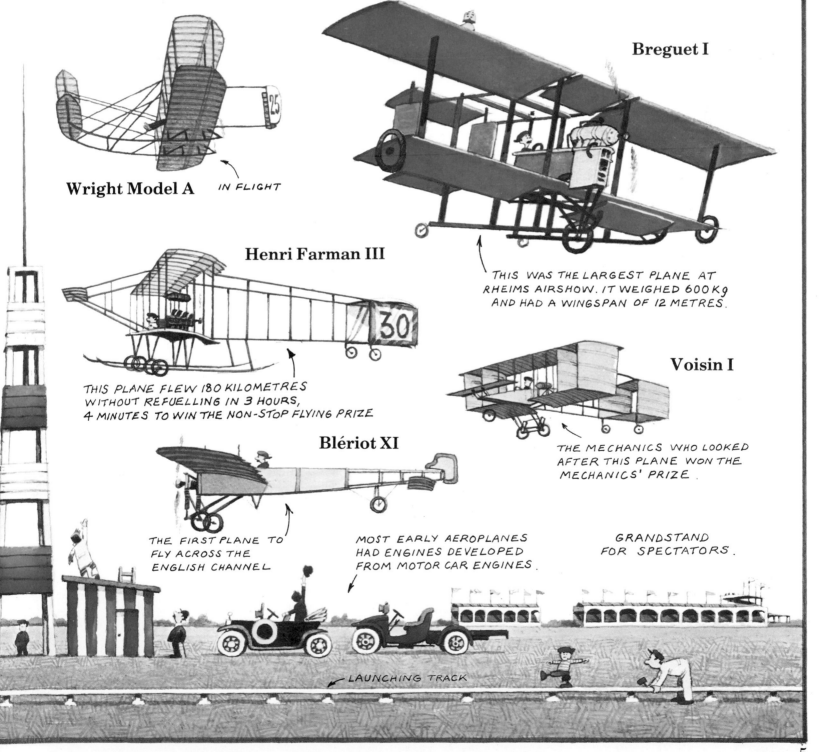

Wright Model A

IN FLIGHT

Breguet I

THIS WAS THE LARGEST PLANE AT RHEIMS AIRSHOW. IT WEIGHED 600 Kg AND HAD A WINGSPAN OF 12 METRES.

Henri Farman III

THIS PLANE FLEW 180 KILOMETRES WITHOUT REFUELLING IN 3 HOURS, 4 MINUTES TO WIN THE NON-STOP FLYING PRIZE

Voisin I

THE MECHANICS WHO LOOKED AFTER THIS PLANE WON THE MECHANICS' PRIZE.

Blériot XI

THE FIRST PLANE TO FLY ACROSS THE ENGLISH CHANNEL

MOST EARLY AEROPLANES HAD ENGINES DEVELOPED FROM MOTOR CAR ENGINES.

GRANDSTAND FOR SPECTATORS.

LAUNCHING TRACK

Fighting in the air

When the First World War started in 1914, most people thought no one would be able to fight in the air. At first, planes were used only for spying and taking photographs. Then pilots began to attack enemy planes too.

Morane Saulnier
This monoplane was made in France. It could fly at 163 kilometres an hour. One pilot tried to catch enemy planes by throwing an anchor at them.

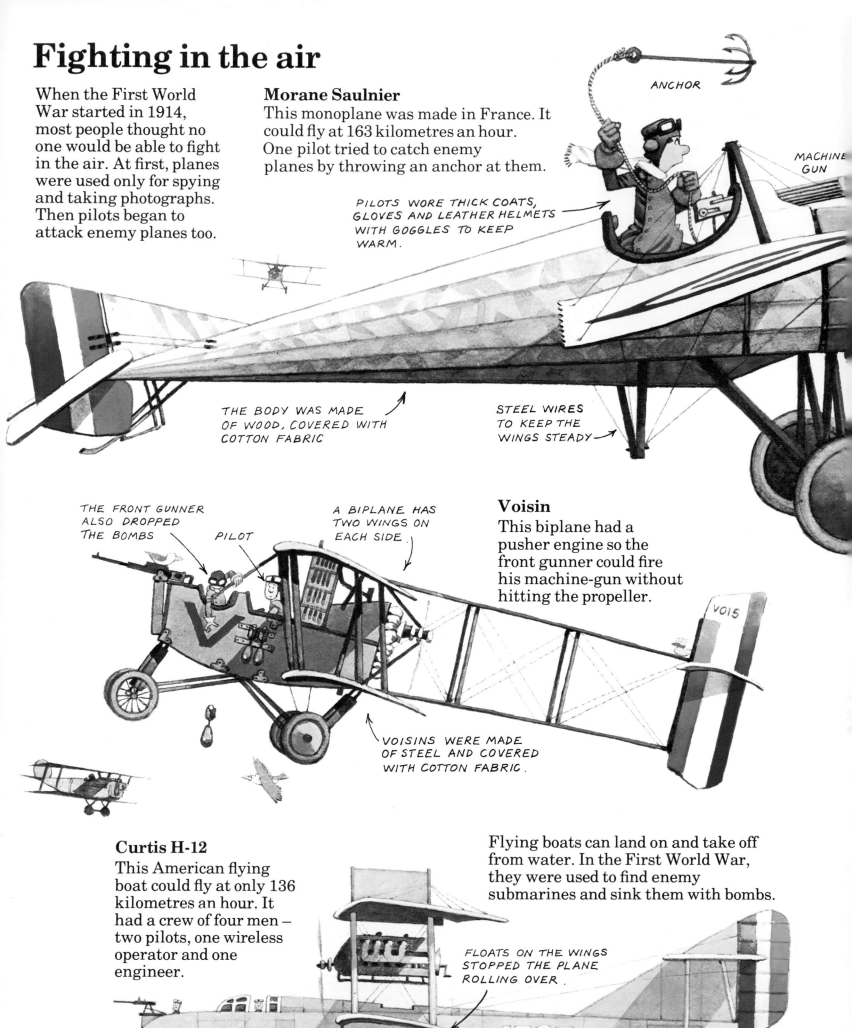

ANCHOR

MACHINE GUN

PILOTS WORE THICK COATS, GLOVES AND LEATHER HELMETS WITH GOGGLES TO KEEP WARM.

THE BODY WAS MADE OF WOOD, COVERED WITH COTTON FABRIC

STEEL WIRES TO KEEP THE WINGS STEADY

THE FRONT GUNNER ALSO DROPPED THE BOMBS

PILOT

A BIPLANE HAS TWO WINGS ON EACH SIDE.

Voisin
This biplane had a pusher engine so the front gunner could fire his machine-gun without hitting the propeller.

VO15

VOISINS WERE MADE OF STEEL AND COVERED WITH COTTON FABRIC.

Curtis H-12
This American flying boat could fly at only 136 kilometres an hour. It had a crew of four men – two pilots, one wireless operator and one engineer.

Flying boats can land on and take off from water. In the First World War, they were used to find enemy submarines and sink them with bombs.

FLOATS ON THE WINGS STOPPED THE PLANE ROLLING OVER.

4767

EXTRA STRONG HULL FOR LANDING ON WATER

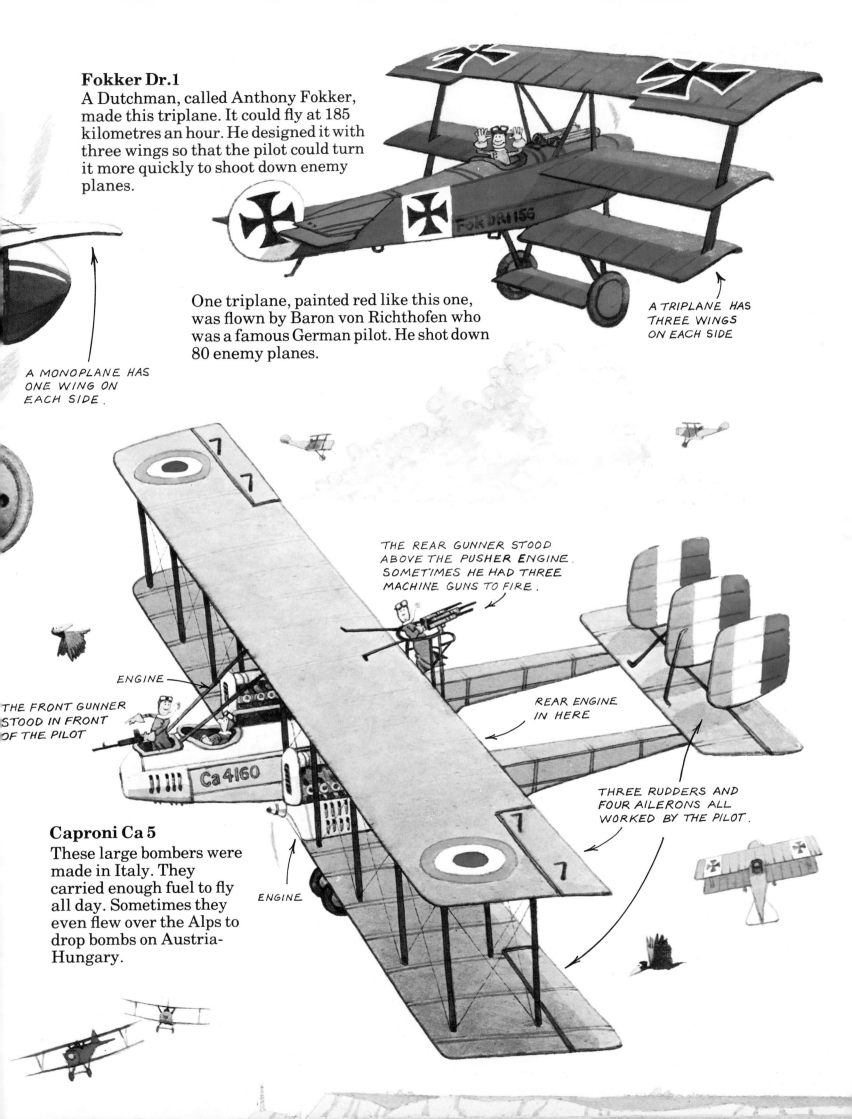

Fokker Dr.1

A Dutchman, called Anthony Fokker, made this triplane. It could fly at 185 kilometres an hour. He designed it with three wings so that the pilot could turn it more quickly to shoot down enemy planes.

One triplane, painted red like this one, was flown by Baron von Richthofen who was a famous German pilot. He shot down 80 enemy planes.

A TRIPLANE HAS THREE WINGS ON EACH SIDE

A MONOPLANE HAS ONE WING ON EACH SIDE.

THE REAR GUNNER STOOD ABOVE THE PUSHER ENGINE. SOMETIMES HE HAD THREE MACHINE GUNS TO FIRE.

ENGINE

THE FRONT GUNNER STOOD IN FRONT OF THE PILOT

REAR ENGINE IN HERE

THREE RUDDERS AND FOUR AILERONS ALL WORKED BY THE PILOT.

Caproni Ca 5

These large bombers were made in Italy. They carried enough fuel to fly all day. Sometimes they even flew over the Alps to drop bombs on Austria-Hungary.

ENGINE

Balloons and airships

Two French brothers, called Montgolfier, invented the first balloon in 1783. They discovered, so the story goes, that hot air rises when they noticed bits of burnt paper flying up from a fire. But they thought it was a special gas.

They worked out that if this was trapped in a big bag, it would float upwards and even be able to carry passengers.

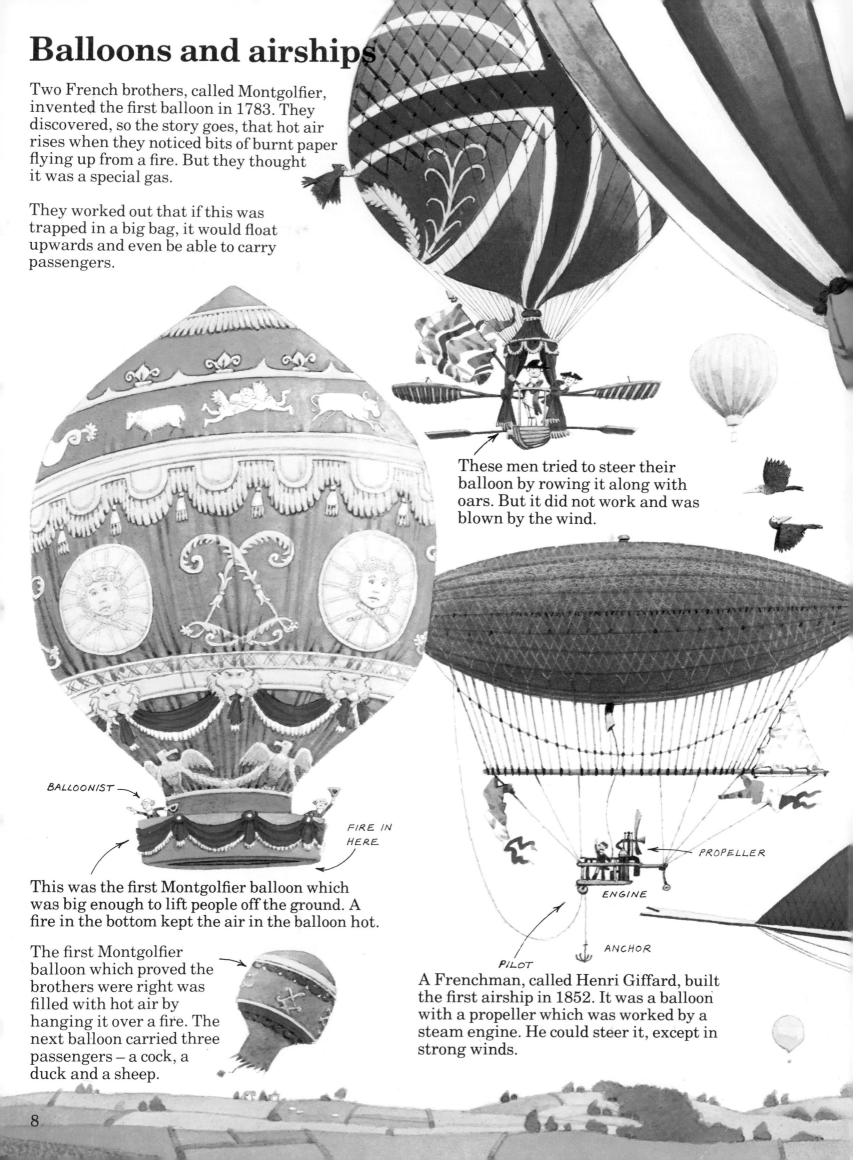

These men tried to steer their balloon by rowing it along with oars. But it did not work and was blown by the wind.

BALLOONIST

FIRE IN HERE

This was the first Montgolfier balloon which was big enough to lift people off the ground. A fire in the bottom kept the air in the balloon hot.

The first Montgolfier balloon which proved the brothers were right was filled with hot air by hanging it over a fire. The next balloon carried three passengers – a cock, a duck and a sheep.

PROPELLER

ENGINE

PILOT

ANCHOR

A Frenchman, called Henri Giffard, built the first airship in 1852. It was a balloon with a propeller which was worked by a steam engine. He could steer it, except in strong winds.

8

ROPES
ATTACHED
TO BALLOON

SILK
SKIN

SAND

GAS BURNER

These 19th century balloonists emptied sandbags to make their balloon lighter. They did this when the balloon was coming down too fast.

A modern high-altitude balloon is full of very light gas. It carries instruments to record the weather and winds high above the Earth.

Modern balloons have a gas burner in the neck. The gas flames heat the air inside the balloon and make it rise off the ground.

This was the first balloon to cross the English Channel. The two men were very cold when they landed. They had thrown away most of their clothes to lighten the balloon and stop it dropping into the sea.

SLIDING WEIGHT

This balloon, like a giant fish, was made in 1804. The captain moved the sliding weight to keep the balloon level.

WINGS TO HELP IT FLY. THEY DID NOT WORK WELL

Amazing aeroplanes

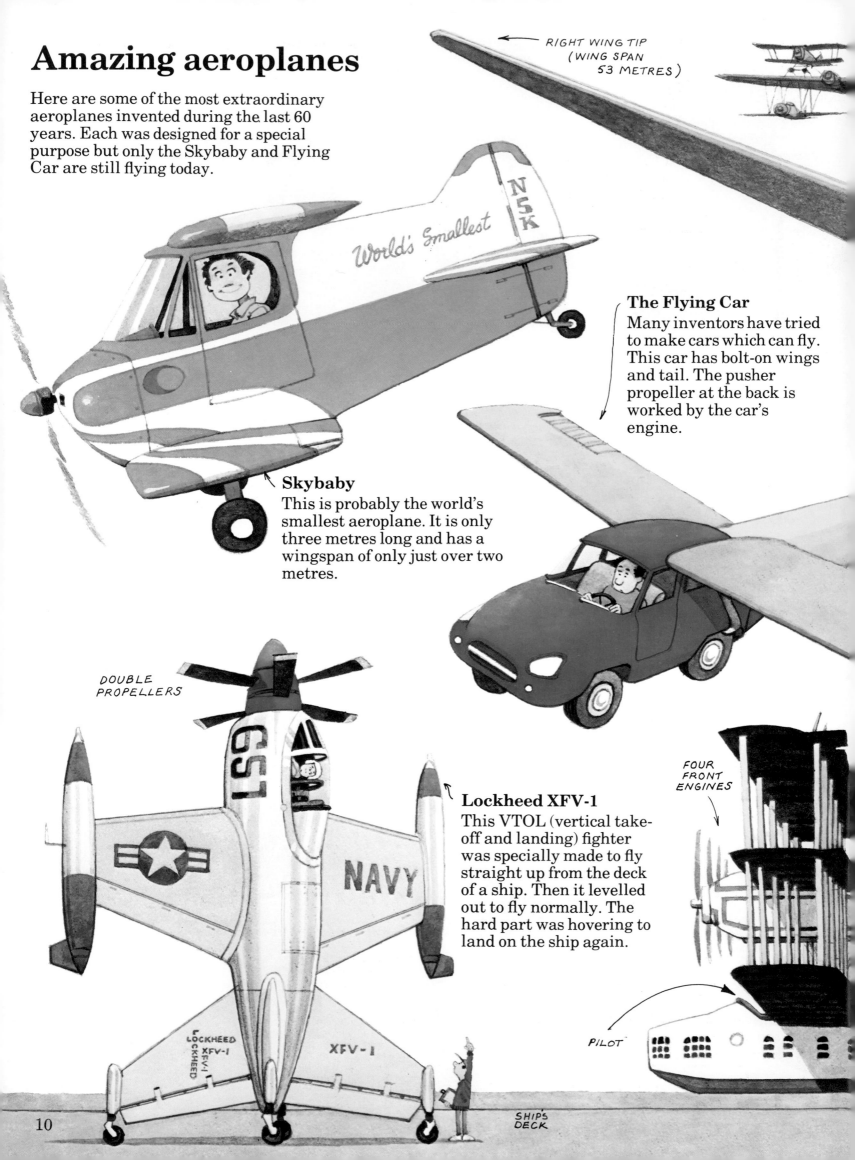

Here are some of the most extraordinary aeroplanes invented during the last 60 years. Each was designed for a special purpose but only the Skybaby and Flying Car are still flying today.

RIGHT WING TIP
(WING SPAN
53 METRES)

World's Smallest

N5K

The Flying Car
Many inventors have tried to make cars which can fly. This car has bolt-on wings and tail. The pusher propeller at the back is worked by the car's engine.

Skybaby
This is probably the world's smallest aeroplane. It is only three metres long and has a wingspan of only just over two metres.

DOUBLE PROPELLERS

FOUR FRONT ENGINES

Lockheed XFV-1
This VTOL (vertical take-off and landing) fighter was specially made to fly straight up from the deck of a ship. Then it levelled out to fly normally. The hard part was hovering to land on the ship again.

NAVY

651

LOCKHEED XFV-1

XFV-1

PILOT

SHIP'S DECK

10

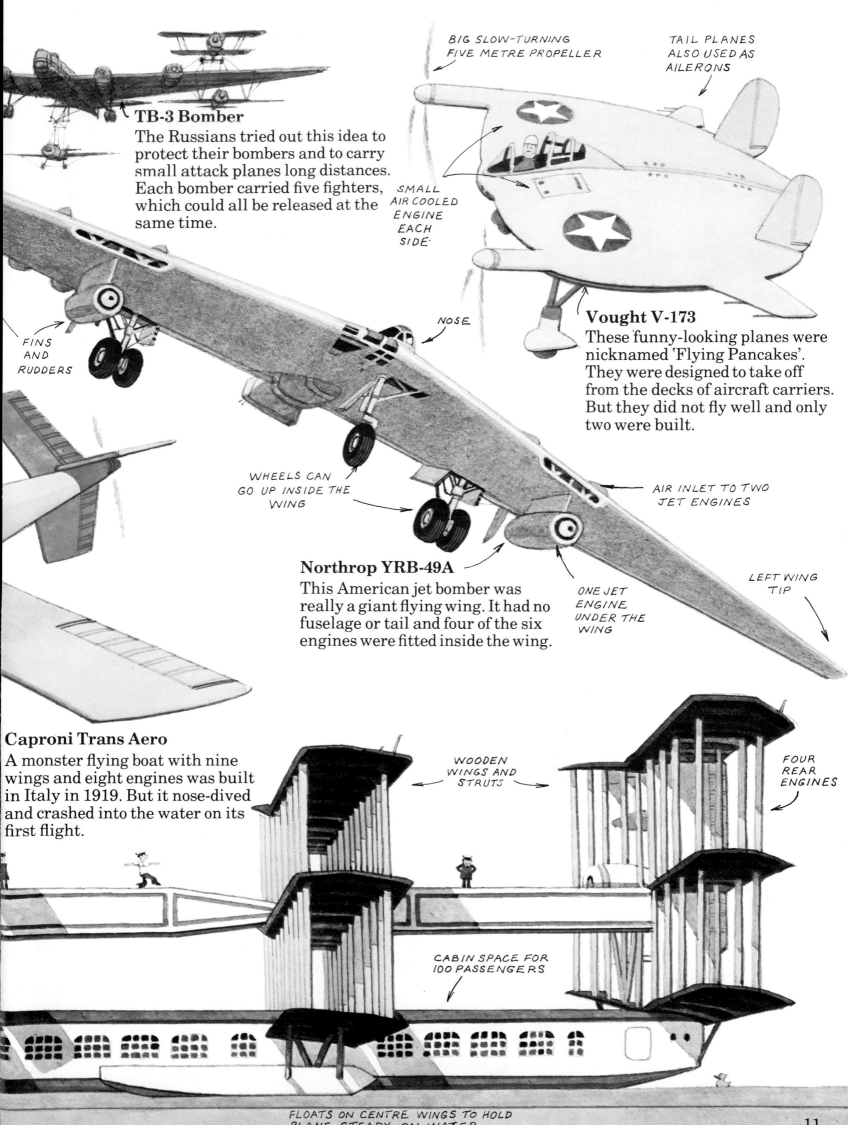

TB-3 Bomber

The Russians tried out this idea to protect their bombers and to carry small attack planes long distances. Each bomber carried five fighters, which could all be released at the same time.

BIG SLOW-TURNING FIVE METRE PROPELLER

TAIL PLANES ALSO USED AS AILERONS

SMALL AIR COOLED ENGINE EACH SIDE.

NOSE

FINS AND RUDDERS

Vought V-173

These funny-looking planes were nicknamed 'Flying Pancakes'. They were designed to take off from the decks of aircraft carriers. But they did not fly well and only two were built.

WHEELS CAN GO UP INSIDE THE WING

AIR INLET TO TWO JET ENGINES

Northrop YRB-49A

This American jet bomber was really a giant flying wing. It had no fuselage or tail and four of the six engines were fitted inside the wing.

ONE JET ENGINE UNDER THE WING

LEFT WING TIP

Caproni Trans Aero

A monster flying boat with nine wings and eight engines was built in Italy in 1919. But it nose-dived and crashed into the water on its first flight.

WOODEN WINGS AND STRUTS

FOUR REAR ENGINES

CABIN SPACE FOR 100 PASSENGERS

FLOATS ON CENTRE WINGS TO HOLD PLANE STEADY ON WATER

Giants of the air

Airship

THE OUTSIDE SKIN IS MADE OF FABRIC

STEEL WIRES TETHER AIRSHIP TO GROUND

PASSENGERS ROOMS

CAPTAIN AT THE HELM

DINING ROOM

LOUNGE

MOTOR

Boeing 747

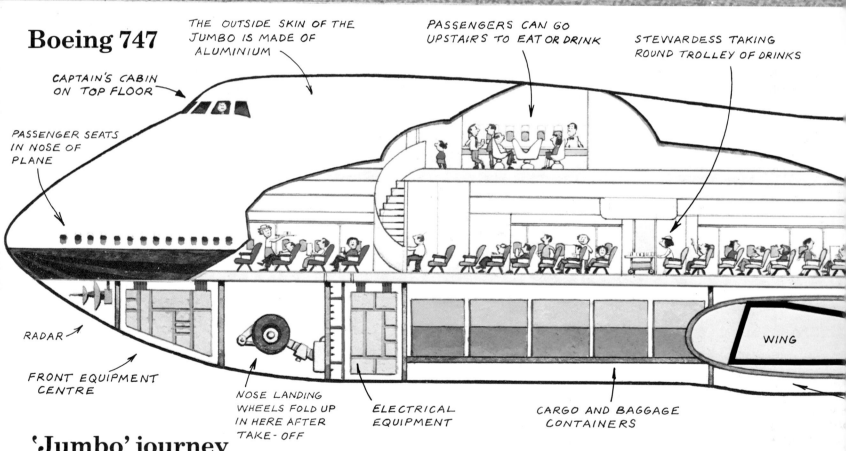

THE OUTSIDE SKIN OF THE JUMBO IS MADE OF ALUMINIUM

PASSENGERS CAN GO UPSTAIRS TO EAT OR DRINK

STEWARDESS TAKING ROUND TROLLEY OF DRINKS

CAPTAIN'S CABIN ON TOP FLOOR

PASSENGER SEATS IN NOSE OF PLANE

RADAR

FRONT EQUIPMENT CENTRE

NOSE LANDING WHEELS FOLD UP IN HERE AFTER TAKE-OFF

ELECTRICAL EQUIPMENT

CARGO AND BAGGAGE CONTAINERS

WING

'Jumbo' journey

1. Mike gives his pass to the stewardess as he walks on board.

2. From his seat he can see the jet's wing and the engines.

3. All the passengers are told to do up their seat belts.

4. Mike is too hot. A stewardess puts his coat in the locker.

5. He has a sweet so his ears will not pop after take-off.

Giant airships, like this one, were more than 200 metres long. The most famous, the Graf Zeppelin, flew round the world in 21 days in 1929.

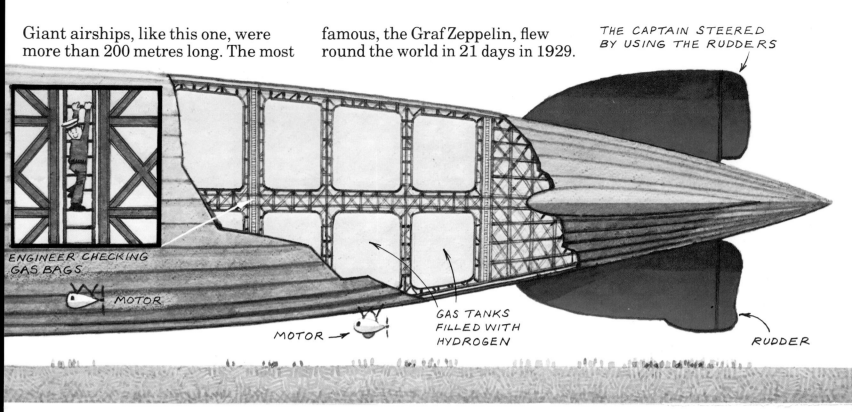

THE CAPTAIN STEERED BY USING THE RUDDERS

ENGINEER CHECKING GAS BAGS

MOTOR

MOTOR →

GAS TANKS FILLED WITH HYDROGEN

RUDDER

This huge jet airliner, called a 'Jumbo' is made by the Boeing Company in America.

It can carry up to 400 passengers and all their luggage across the Atlantic in less than seven hours.

Special cargo Jumbos can carry up to 113 tonnes. Their noses open and swing upwards to load the cargo.

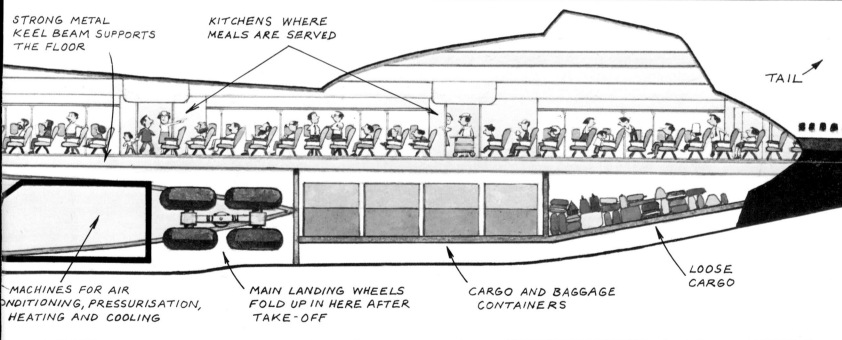

STRONG METAL KEEL BEAM SUPPORTS THE FLOOR

KITCHENS WHERE MEALS ARE SERVED

TAIL

MACHINES FOR AIR CONDITIONING, PRESSURISATION, HEATING AND COOLING

MAIN LANDING WHEELS FOLD UP IN HERE AFTER TAKE-OFF

CARGO AND BAGGAGE CONTAINERS

LOOSE CARGO

6

7

8

9

10

The engines are very noisy as the Jumbo jet takes off.

Mike is still too hot. He turns a knob to get some cool air.

Lunch is served on a tray. Mike is hungry and eats it all.

He plugs in his earphones and hears some music.

The plane is like a flying hotel. It even has lavatories.

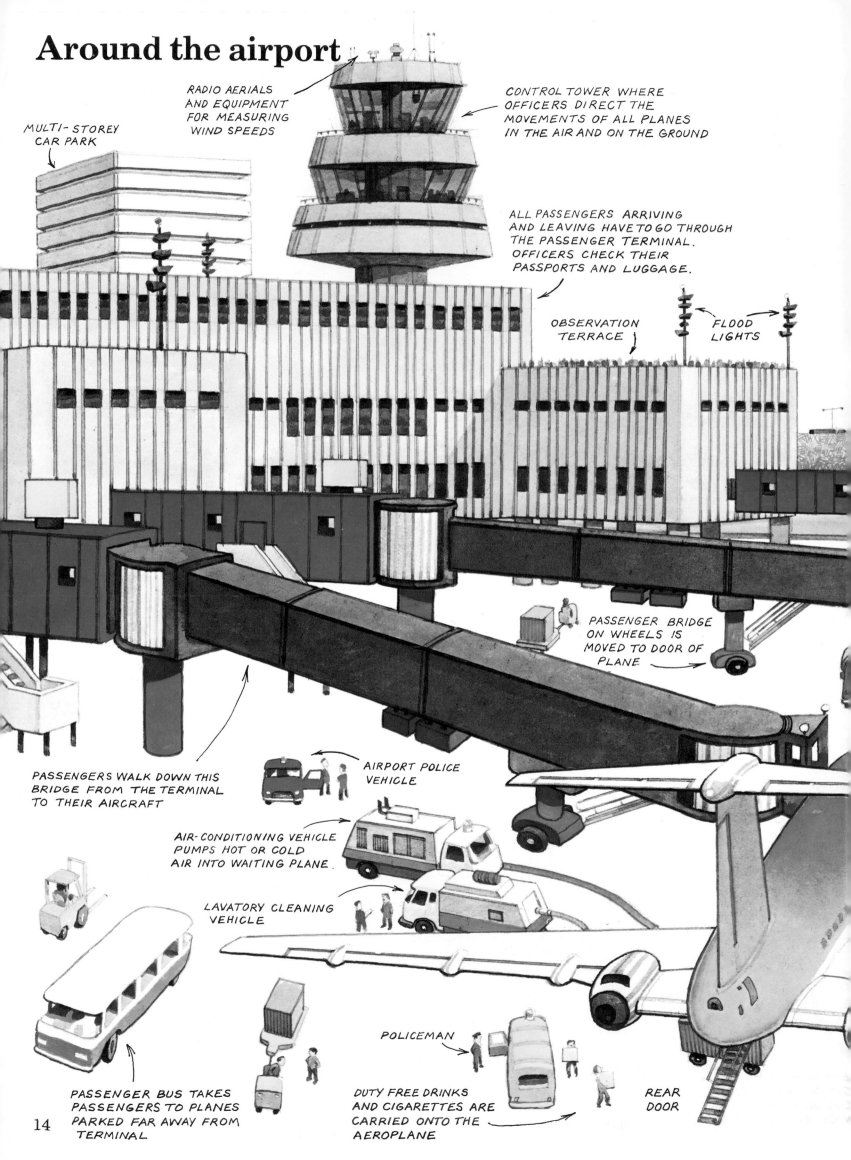

Around the airport

RADIO AERIALS AND EQUIPMENT FOR MEASURING WIND SPEEDS

CONTROL TOWER WHERE OFFICERS DIRECT THE MOVEMENTS OF ALL PLANES IN THE AIR AND ON THE GROUND

MULTI-STOREY CAR PARK

ALL PASSENGERS ARRIVING AND LEAVING HAVE TO GO THROUGH THE PASSENGER TERMINAL. OFFICERS CHECK THEIR PASSPORTS AND LUGGAGE.

OBSERVATION TERRACE

FLOOD LIGHTS

PASSENGER BRIDGE ON WHEELS IS MOVED TO DOOR OF PLANE

PASSENGERS WALK DOWN THIS BRIDGE FROM THE TERMINAL TO THEIR AIRCRAFT

AIRPORT POLICE VEHICLE

AIR-CONDITIONING VEHICLE PUMPS HOT OR COLD AIR INTO WAITING PLANE.

LAVATORY CLEANING VEHICLE

POLICEMAN

DUTY FREE DRINKS AND CIGARETTES ARE CARRIED ONTO THE AEROPLANE

REAR DOOR

PASSENGER BUS TAKES PASSENGERS TO PLANES PARKED FAR AWAY FROM TERMINAL

14

PLANES HAVE TO WAIT TO LAND
WHEN THE AIRPORT IS VERY BUSY
PILOTS ARE TOLD BY THE CONTROL
TOWER TO FLY ROUND AT CERTAIN
HEIGHTS. THIS IS CALLED 'STACKING'

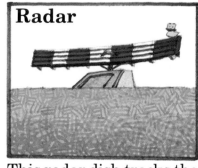

Radar

This radar dish tracks the flight of all planes flying near the airport.

A300 AIRBUS TAKING OFF

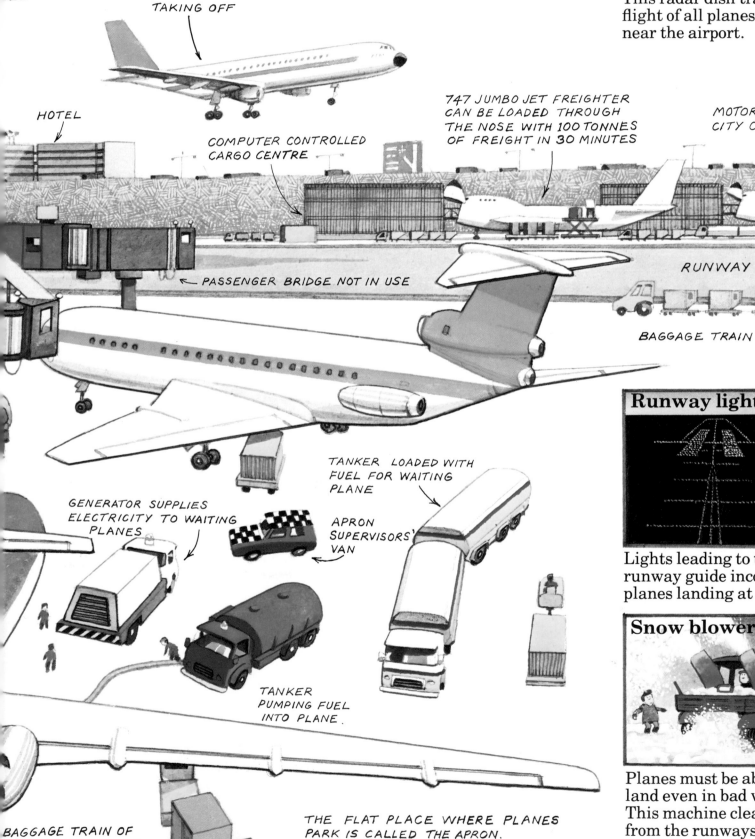

HOTEL

COMPUTER CONTROLLED CARGO CENTRE

747 JUMBO JET FREIGHTER CAN BE LOADED THROUGH THE NOSE WITH 100 TONNES OF FREIGHT IN 30 MINUTES

MOTORWAY TO CITY CENTRE

PASSENGER BRIDGE NOT IN USE

RUNWAY

BAGGAGE TRAIN

Runway lights

Lights leading to the runway guide incoming planes landing at night.

GENERATOR SUPPLIES ELECTRICITY TO WAITING PLANES

TANKER LOADED WITH FUEL FOR WAITING PLANE

APRON SUPERVISORS' VAN

TANKER PUMPING FUEL INTO PLANE.

Snow blower

Planes must be able to land even in bad weather. This machine clears snow from the runways.

BAGGAGE TRAIN OF CONTAINERS FULL OF LUGGAGE FOR WIDE-BODIED JET

THE FLAT PLACE WHERE PLANES PARK IS CALLED THE APRON. AIRCRAFT FUEL IS STORED IN GIANT TANKS UNDER THE APRON.

Prepare for take-off

1

Three hours before a plane takes off, the captain and his crew arrive at the airport in an airline bus. They have a lot of work to do.

2

They write a flight plan, showing which route they will use and their height.

They carefully check weather reports and runway conditions.

3

Fuel is pumped from huge underground tanks into the plane.

The main fuel tanks are in the wings of large jet airliners.

4

Engineers have already tested the plane very carefully. On their way

out the flight crew check everything again, just to make sure.

5

In the cockpit they check all the instruments. It takes a long time.

They make sure all the systems to control the plane work.

6

When Passenger Mike goes to the airport, he has his suitcase weighed.

7

Then a porter packs his case in a container which is loaded on to the plane.

8

At Passport Control Mike shows his passport. It is stamped.

9

Alarms will ring on this security machine if he has any weapons.

10

Mike looks at the Destination Board in the departure lounge.

It shows when all the planes will take off and their flight numbers.

11

When Mike's plane is ready, he is allowed to choose his seat.

12

He walks down a long passenger bridge to the door of the plane.

13

The doors are shut when everyone is sitting in their seats.

On the flight deck, the Captain and crew have finished their checks.

14

Then the Captain talks over the radio to the Control Tower.

15

Control checks that no planes are moving on to the runway.

16

A marshaller stands on the ground, giving signals to the Captain.

17

He wears ear muffs or he would be deafened by the noise of the engines.

18

A small tractor pushes the huge plane out of its parking place.

19

Control gives the Captain permission to taxi away across the airport.

He checks the radar screen and looks out of the window of the Tower.

20

The Captain steers the plane to the runway and joins the take-off queue.

21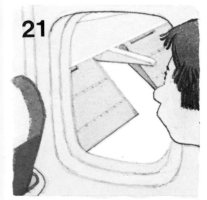

Mike watches the wing flaps move down into position for take-off.

22

The engines are very noisy as the jet speeds down the runway.

Suddenly it tilts upwards and rises smoothly into the air. They are off.

23

When the plane reaches its flying height, the Captain visits the cabin.

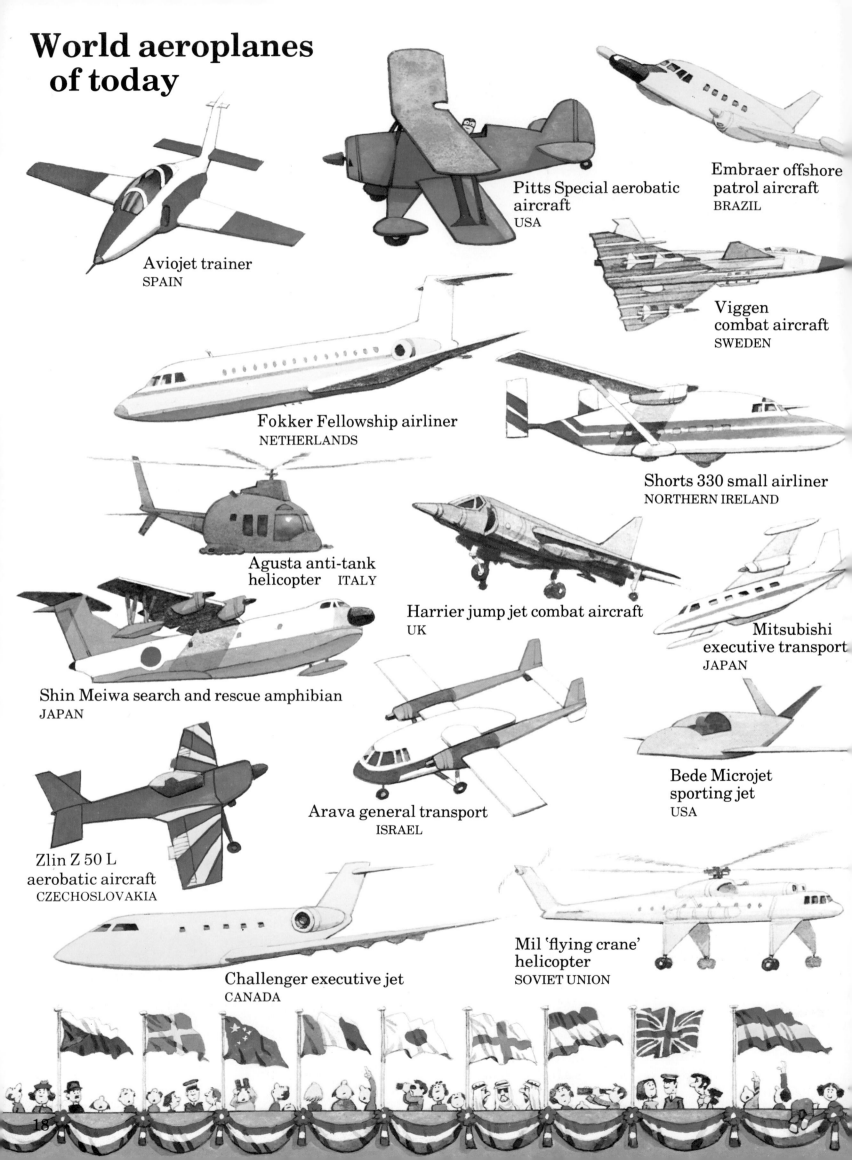

World aeroplanes of today

Aviojet trainer
SPAIN

Pitts Special aerobatic aircraft
USA

Embraer offshore patrol aircraft
BRAZIL

Viggen combat aircraft
SWEDEN

Fokker Fellowship airliner
NETHERLANDS

Shorts 330 small airliner
NORTHERN IRELAND

Agusta anti-tank helicopter   ITALY

Harrier jump jet combat aircraft
UK

Mitsubishi executive transport
JAPAN

Shin Meiwa search and rescue amphibian
JAPAN

Arava general transport
ISRAEL

Bede Microjet sporting jet
USA

Zlin Z 50 L aerobatic aircraft
CZECHOSLOVAKIA

Challenger executive jet
CANADA

Mil 'flying crane' helicopter
SOVIET UNION

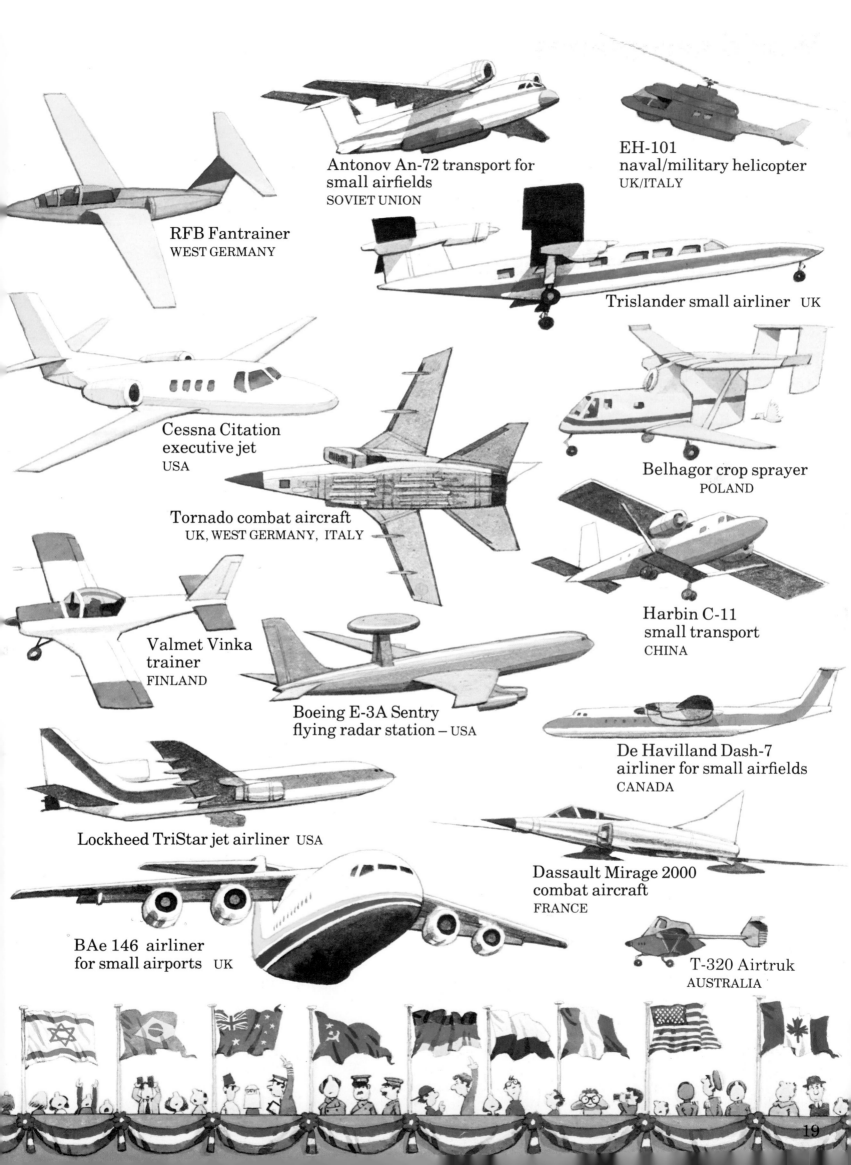

Antonov An-72 transport for small airfields
SOVIET UNION

EH-101 naval/military helicopter
UK/ITALY

RFB Fantrainer
WEST GERMANY

Trislander small airliner UK

Cessna Citation executive jet
USA

Belhagor crop sprayer
POLAND

Tornado combat aircraft
UK, WEST GERMANY, ITALY

Valmet Vinka trainer
FINLAND

Boeing E-3A Sentry flying radar station – USA

Harbin C-11 small transport
CHINA

De Havilland Dash-7 airliner for small airfields
CANADA

Lockheed TriStar jet airliner USA

Dassault Mirage 2000 combat aircraft
FRANCE

BAe 146 airliner for small airports UK

T-320 Airtruk
AUSTRALIA

Helicopters

The first helicopter was built in France in 1907. Helpers had to hold it down on the ground to stop it flying out of control.

This VS-300 was the first real helicopter to fly properly. It was built by Igor Sikorsky in America in 1939.

Two years later, Sikorsky built the world's first useful helicopter. This was the two-seater R-4 which was used in the Second World War.

Parts of a helicopter

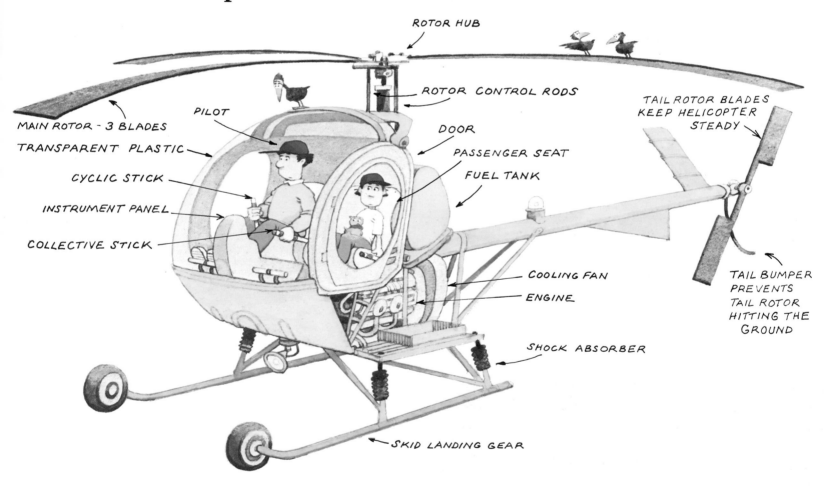

ROTOR HUB

ROTOR CONTROL RODS

TAIL ROTOR BLADES KEEP HELICOPTER STEADY

MAIN ROTOR - 3 BLADES

PILOT

DOOR

TRANSPARENT PLASTIC

PASSENGER SEAT

CYCLIC STICK

FUEL TANK

INSTRUMENT PANEL

COLLECTIVE STICK

COOLING FAN

ENGINE

TAIL BUMPER PREVENTS TAIL ROTOR HITTING THE GROUND

SHOCK ABSORBER

SKID LANDING GEAR

Flying a helicopter

This simple helicopter is used for training pilots. The rotor blades on top lift it off the ground and pull it through the air.

The pilot raises and lowers the collective stick to make the helicopter go up and down. He twists the end to rev the engine.

He holds the cyclic stick in his right hand and moves it backwards or forwards or sideways to make the helicopter change direction.

Modern helicopters, like this BO 105 can fly very fast and are easy to control in the air.

Police sometimes use them to watch traffic and even follow the cars of escaping criminals.

This Chinook helicopter is named after a Red Indian tribe. It has two lifting rotors.

It can lift ten tonnes of cargo or carry 44 passengers at a speed of 250 kilometres per hour.

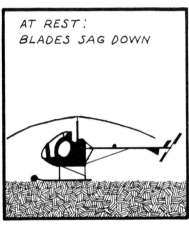

AT REST: BLADES SAG DOWN

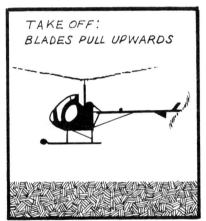

TAKE OFF: BLADES PULL UPWARDS

TO GO AHEAD: BLADES TILT FORWARD

TO GO SIDEWAYS: BLADES TILT SIDEWAYS

TO STOP OR GO BACKWARDS: BLADES TILT BACK

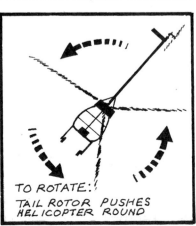

TO ROTATE: TAIL ROTOR PUSHES HELICOPTER ROUND

This giant helicopter is called a Skycrane. It can lift a load weighing up to ten tonnes.

Skycranes are used to move loads which are too big to be carried by a train or lorry.

Learning to fly

When a pilot is learning to fly, he flies a two-seater plane with two sets of controls. The learner has one set and the instructor has the other. This little plane has only one seat and is used for practising.

All planes have hinged parts on the tail and wings. They are called elevators, ailerons and the rudder.

The pilot steers the plane by moving these parts. They are joined by wires to the pilot's controls in the cockpit.

He uses the control column (stick) to move the elevators and ailerons, and he presses the foot pedals to move the rudder.

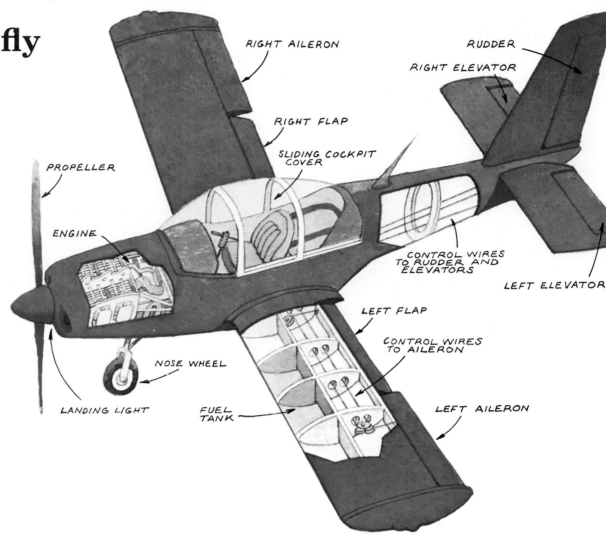

PROPELLER

ENGINE

LANDING LIGHT

NOSE WHEEL

FUEL TANK

RIGHT AILERON

RIGHT FLAP

SLIDING COCKPIT COVER

RUDDER

RIGHT ELEVATOR

CONTROL WIRES TO RUDDER AND ELEVATORS

LEFT ELEVATOR

LEFT FLAP

CONTROL WIRES TO AILERON

LEFT AILERON

1 Taking off

THROTTLE FORWARD

The pilot straps himself in and is ready for take off. He pushes the throttle lever forward to give the engine more power.

2

CONTROL COLUMN BACK

He watches the air speed indicator to see when the plane is moving fast enough along the ground. Then he pulls back the control column (stick).

3

ELEVATORS UP

This moves the elevators up. The air passing over them pushes the tail down so the nose rises, and the plane takes off.

Using elevators

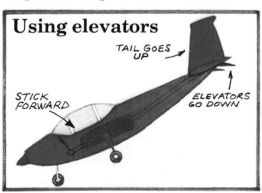

TAIL GOES UP

STICK FORWARD

ELEVATORS GO DOWN

In the air, if the pilot pushes the stick forward, the elevators move down. The air pushes the tail up and the plane dives.

Using ailerons

RIGHT AILERON DOWN

LEFT AILERON UP

If the pilot moves the stick to the left, the left aileron goes up and the right one goes down. The plane then rolls to the left.

Using the rudder

TAIL SWINGS TO THE RIGHT

If he pushes the left rudder pedal down, the rudder moves to the left. This pushes the tail to the right, and turns the plane to the left.

In the cockpit

The cockpit might look like this. Once he is in the air, the pilot controls the plane mainly with the stick and rudder pedals. He will use the throttle if he wants to go faster or to climb, and he must watch all his instruments carefully, especially when he is turning, taking off or landing.

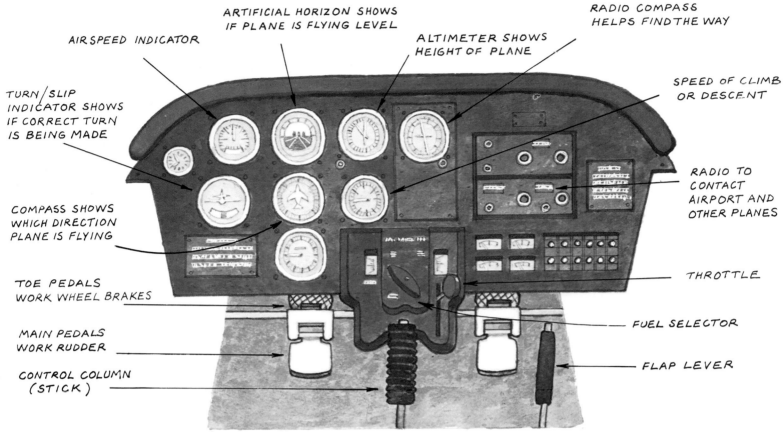

AIR SPEED INDICATOR

ARTIFICIAL HORIZON SHOWS IF PLANE IS FLYING LEVEL

ALTIMETER SHOWS HEIGHT OF PLANE

RADIO COMPASS HELPS FIND THE WAY

TURN/SLIP INDICATOR SHOWS IF CORRECT TURN IS BEING MADE

SPEED OF CLIMB OR DESCENT

COMPASS SHOWS WHICH DIRECTION PLANE IS FLYING

RADIO TO CONTACT AIRPORT AND OTHER PLANES

TOE PEDALS WORK WHEEL BRAKES

THROTTLE

MAIN PEDALS WORK RUDDER

FUEL SELECTOR

CONTROL COLUMN (STICK)

FLAP LEVER

Turning

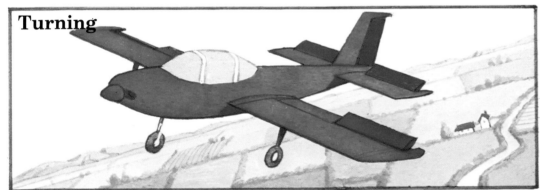

To make a correct turn, the pilot must use all three controls – elevators, ailerons and rudder. He moves the stick to one side to make the plane roll. At the same time, he pulls back on the stick and pushes the rudder pedal to swing the tail round.

Turning sharply

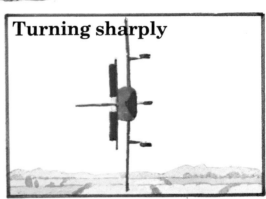

Only an experienced pilot would turn as sharply as this. He is pulling so hard on the stick, the wings are sideways to the ground.

1 Landing

THROTTLE BACK

STICK FORWARD

FLAP LEVER

The pilot closes the throttle and pushes the stick forward to make the plane glide down. Then he pulls up the flap lever.

2

FLAPS DOWN

Now the flaps on both wings are down. The air rushing over them helps to slow the plane down and land in a short distance.

3

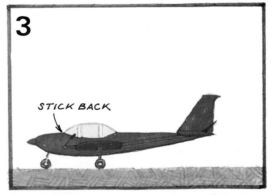

STICK BACK

As the plane comes down to land, the pilot keeps pulling back on the stick until all the wheels are on the ground. Then he taxis to a halt.

23

Aerobatics

Some pilots do aerobatics for fun or to give displays at airshows. Others are taught aerobatics to help them become better pilots.

This Swedish Safari two-seater plane is flying 'round the houses'. Low flying is not often allowed, especially near buildings.

Wing-walking is an exciting stunt at airshows. Biplanes fitted with special attachments on the top wing are often used.

Aerobatics are often done by several planes flying together. These three biplanes are streaming out special coloured smoke.

Tape cutting

This is daredevil flying to thrill a crowd at an airshow. The pilot flies just above the ground so that the propeller of his plane cuts a tape held between two long poles. Just to make it harder, the pilot sometimes flies upside down.

Doing a roll

1 The plane | **2** | **3** | **4** | **5**

What the pilot sees

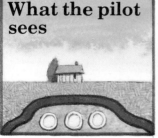  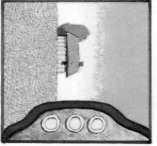 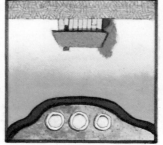 

The plane is level with the ground.

Now it begins to roll to the left.

Quarter way round. It is on its side.

Halfway round. Upside down.

All the way round. Level again.

Formation flying

A group of aeroplanes, controlled by a leader, can fly in lots of different formations. 'Line Ahead' means they fly in a line, one behind the other. 'Line Abreast' means all in one line, side by side. 'V Formation' means all the aeroplanes fly in the shape of the letter V with the leader at the front.

This team is the RAF's Red Arrows. They are doing a spectacular manoeuvre called a 'Bomb Burst'. Each aeroplane is trailing coloured smoke so watchers on the ground can see them more easily.

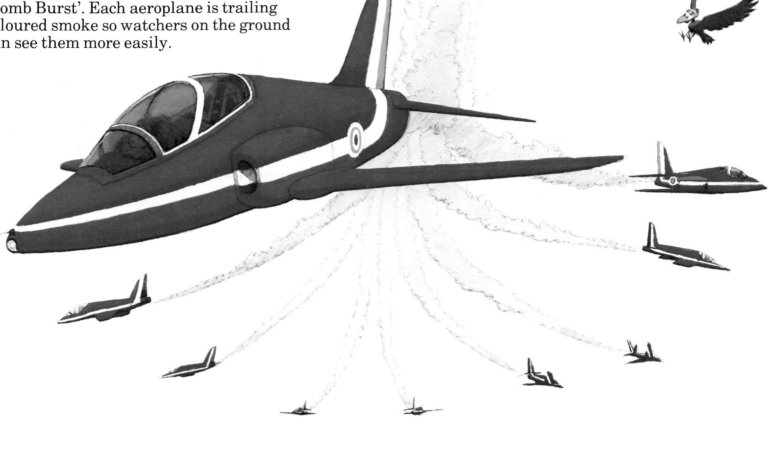

A stall turn

A loop

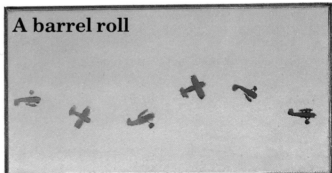

A barrel roll

A vertical 8

Hang gliding

Hang gliding is an exciting and quite cheap sport. Flyers carry their gliders, folded up, to the top of a steep hill. Then they fit the glider together, strap themselves on and launch off into the wind. If a strong wind is blowing up the hill, they can climb very high and stay up for hours.

ENGINE

THIS HANG GLIDER HAS BEEN FITTED WITH AN ENGINE SO THE FLYER DOES NOT HAVE TO WAIT FOR A GOOD WIND.

CRASH HELMET

WARM CLOTHES

SKILLED HANG GLIDERS LIE FLAT LIKE THIS ONE THEY CAN ALSO STEER BY MOVING THEIR BODIES FROM SIDE TO SIDE

BOOTS

THE WINGS ARE MADE FROM THIN NYLON FABRIC. AIR TRAPPED BENEATH THEM MAKES THEM BULGE UPWARDS THIS MAKES THE HANG GLIDER FLY

DOUBLE HANG GLIDER

LIGHT ALUMINIUM TUBE

STEEL WIRES

Francis Rogallo invented the first hang glider in America. Developed and improved, they have been used for dropping heavy loads from aeroplanes and recovering spacecraft.

Launching a hang glider

1 Climbing up the hill. Hang glider is folded up.

2 On top of the hill. Fit it together.

3 Helmet on. Face the wind. Run down slope to launch.

4 Up in the air at last. Floating gently around.

Gliding

Gliders are very light with long wings. They have no engines. This special one is called a sailplane.

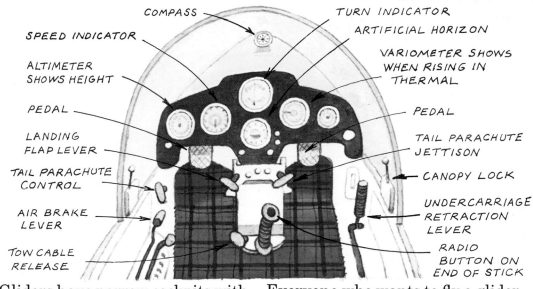

COMPASS

SPEED INDICATOR

TURN INDICATOR

ARTIFICIAL HORIZON

ALTIMETER SHOWS HEIGHT

VARIOMETER SHOWS WHEN RISING IN THERMAL

PEDAL

PEDAL

LANDING FLAP LEVER

TAIL PARACHUTE JETTISON

TAIL PARACHUTE CONTROL

CANOPY LOCK

AIR BRAKE LEVER

UNDERCARRIAGE RETRACTION LEVER

TOW CABLE RELEASE

RADIO BUTTON ON END OF STICK

Gliders have narrow cockpits with nearly as many instruments and controls as a small powered plane.

Everyone who wants to fly a glider must first have lessons in a two-seater glider with an instructor.

1 Launching a glider

Gliders can be winched into the air, towed by a car, or towed up by an aeroplane, like this one.

2

The glider is just off the ground. The pilot has maps, food and drink. His flight may last all day.

3

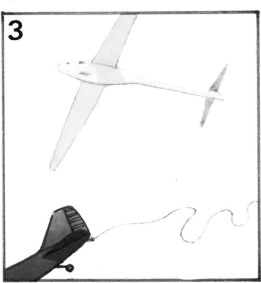

When the pilot has his glider in a good position, he releases the tow cable. Now he is on his own.

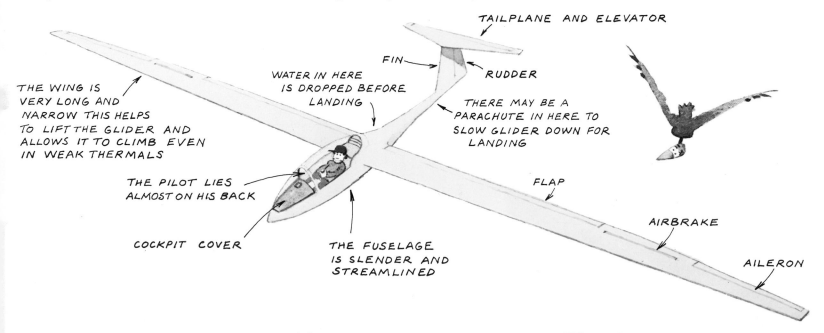

TAILPLANE AND ELEVATOR

FIN

RUDDER

WATER IN HERE IS DROPPED BEFORE LANDING

THERE MAY BE A PARACHUTE IN HERE TO SLOW GLIDER DOWN FOR LANDING

THE WING IS VERY LONG AND NARROW THIS HELPS TO LIFT THE GLIDER AND ALLOWS IT TO CLIMB EVEN IN WEAK THERMALS

THE PILOT LIES ALMOST ON HIS BACK

FLAP

COCKPIT COVER

THE FUSELAGE IS SLENDER AND STREAMLINED

AIRBRAKE

AILERON

Columns of warm rising air, called thermals, lift gliders higher and higher in the sky. Skilled glider pilots know where to find them.

After rising on a thermal, the pilot lowers the nose of his glider and races down to the next one. Then he begins to climb again.

When the pilot has to land, he drops the water ballast and lowers the landing wheel. When he is nearly down, he opens the airbrakes.

Rockets and spacecraft

The first rockets were probably made long ago in China. Nobody knows how well they actually worked.

Naval rocket

About 170 years ago, the British army fired gunpowder rockets at the French army, led by Napoleon. Some, like this one, were launched from boats.

V2 Rocket

By the Second World War, much bigger rockets, using liquid fuel, had been invented. They could fly 350 kilometres.

This is a German V-2 rocket. Thousands like this were fired at London from hidden trailers in France and Holland.

Sputnik

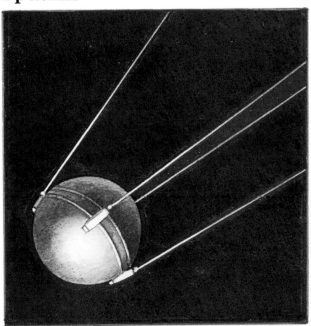

By 1950, scientists were planning space flights. On 4 October, 1957, the Soviet Union fired the first satellite into orbit round the world. It was called Sputnik 1.

Vostok 1

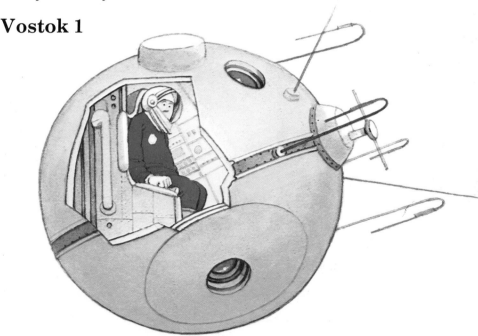

The Russians were also the first to put a man in space. This was more difficult because he needed an air-conditioned capsule and a way of getting back to Earth. Vostok 1 was launched in 1961. The cosmonaut was Yuri Gagarin.

Apollo Mission

Soon after Vostok 1 was launched, the Americans joined the 'space race'. President Kennedy said that an American would walk on the Moon within ten years.

The Americans built the world's biggest rocket. It was called Saturn V and was 110 metres high.

In July, 1969, Saturn V blasted off from Cape Canaveral. It carried three astronauts, Neil Armstrong, 'Buzz' Aldrin and Michael Collins, into orbit round the Moon.

Armstrong and Aldrin then landed the Lunar Module on the Moon while Collins stayed in orbit. After 21 hours, the two men blasted off in part of the Lunar Module and linked up again with Collins.

Saturn Rocket

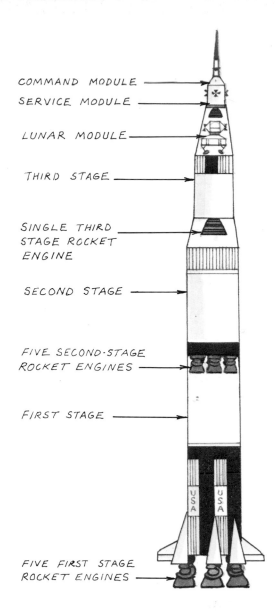

COMMAND MODULE
SERVICE MODULE
LUNAR MODULE
THIRD STAGE
SINGLE THIRD STAGE ROCKET ENGINE
SECOND STAGE
FIVE SECOND-STAGE ROCKET ENGINES
FIRST STAGE
FIVE FIRST STAGE ROCKET ENGINES

Apollo Command Module

The three Apollo astronauts lived and worked in this pressurised Command Module during most of their Moon flight. It was the only part of the Saturn rocket to return to Earth. At the end of the journey, the astronauts floated down by parachute in the Command Module and landed in the Pacific.

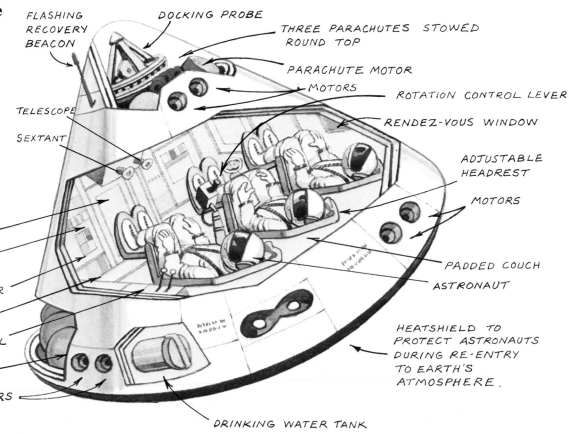

FLASHING RECOVERY BEACON
DOCKING PROBE
THREE PARACHUTES STOWED ROUND TOP
PARACHUTE MOTOR
MOTORS
ROTATION CONTROL LEVER
RENDEZ-VOUS WINDOW
TELESCOPE
SEXTANT
ADJUSTABLE HEADREST
MOTORS
GUIDANCE AND NAVIGATION CONTROL
LIGHTING CONTROL
FOOD LOCKER
CABIN PRESSURE CONTROL
OXYGEN CONTROL
FUEL TANKS
MOTORS
PADDED COUCH
ASTRONAUT
HEATSHIELD TO PROTECT ASTRONAUTS DURING RE-ENTRY TO EARTH'S ATMOSPHERE.
DRINKING WATER TANK

The Space Shuttle

The Shuttle is launched, standing on its tail, from Cape Kennedy.

Just 122 seconds after lift-off, the giant boost motors separate.

The fuel tanks separate 114 kilometres above the Earth.

Now two small engines take the Shuttle Orbiter into its orbit.

Shuttles working in space

All space launches up to 1980 have been made with rockets that could only be used once.

Now American scientists have invented the Space Shuttle which can be used over and over again. The pictures along the top of this page show how the Shuttle Orbiter blasts into space and comes back.

Here are some different space jobs which could be done by Space Shuttles.

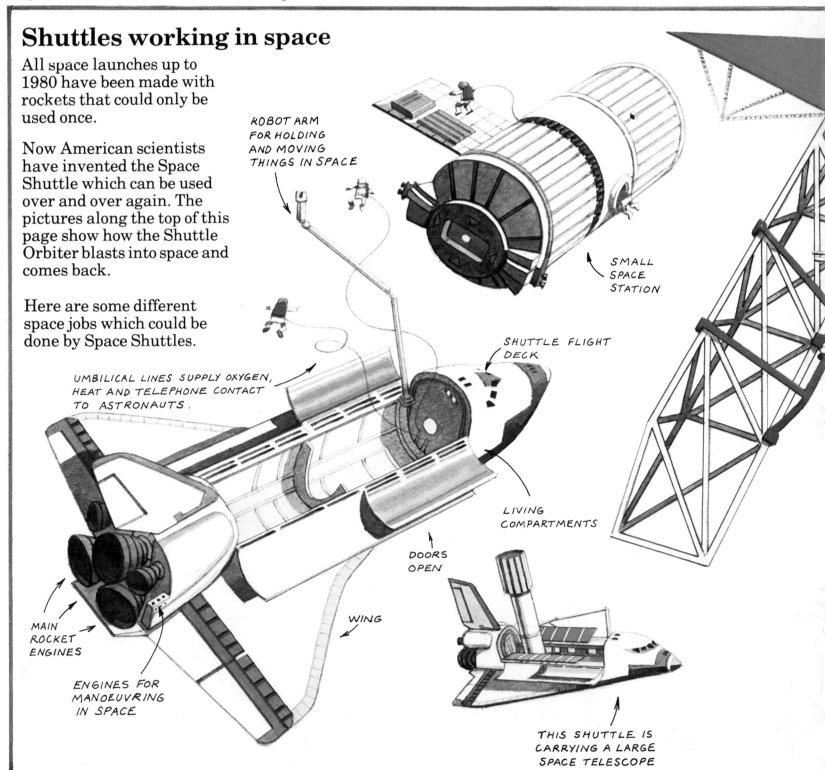

ROBOT ARM FOR HOLDING AND MOVING THINGS IN SPACE

SMALL SPACE STATION

SHUTTLE FLIGHT DECK

UMBILICAL LINES SUPPLY OXYGEN, HEAT AND TELEPHONE CONTACT TO ASTRONAUTS.

LIVING COMPARTMENTS

MAIN ROCKET ENGINES

DOORS OPEN

WING

ENGINES FOR MANOEUVRING IN SPACE

THIS SHUTTLE IS CARRYING A LARGE SPACE TELESCOPE

The payload bay is open. This mission's cargo is taken out.

Later the Shuttle Orbiter comes back to Earth glowing red hot.

Now it flies like an aeroplane and makes a normal landing.

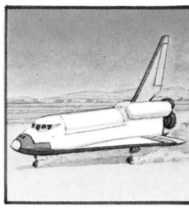

Soon the Shuttle Orbiter will be ready for its next mission into space.

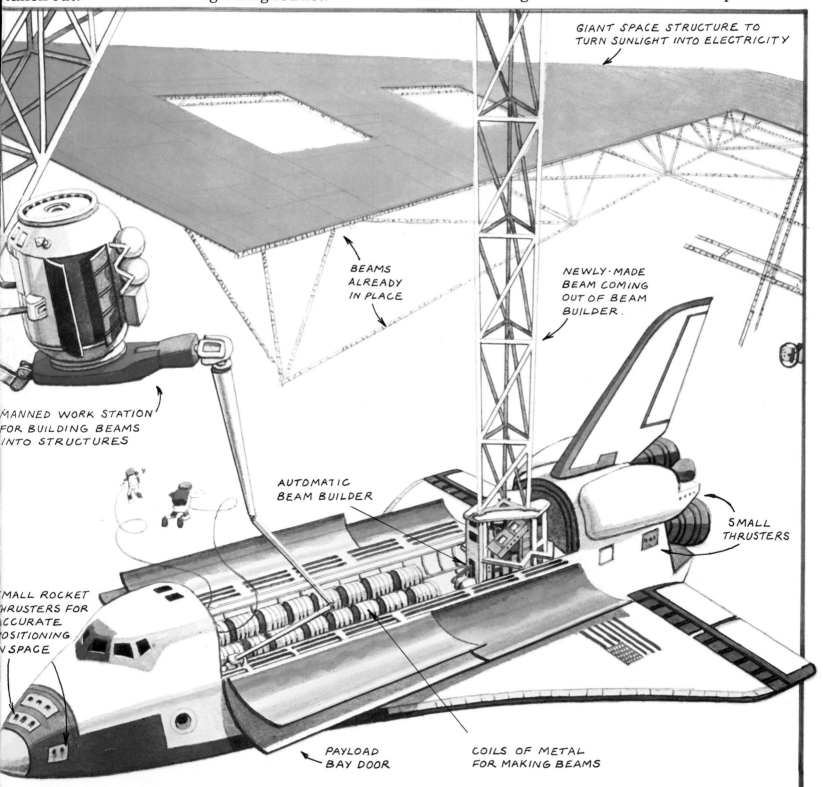

GIANT SPACE STRUCTURE TO TURN SUNLIGHT INTO ELECTRICITY

BEAMS ALREADY IN PLACE

NEWLY-MADE BEAM COMING OUT OF BEAM BUILDER.

MANNED WORK STATION FOR BUILDING BEAMS INTO STRUCTURES

AUTOMATIC BEAM BUILDER

SMALL THRUSTERS

SMALL ROCKET THRUSTERS FOR ACCURATE POSITIONING IN SPACE

PAYLOAD BAY DOOR

COILS OF METAL FOR MAKING BEAMS

Flying facts and feats

Longest pedal flight

For many years, people have tried to build aeroplanes that they could fly just by pedalling them.

This is the Gossamer Albatross. It is very light and has extremely long wings to keep it in the air.

An American, Bryan Allen, pedalled it from England to France in 1979, in 2 hours 49 minutes.

Longest fall

An American officer jumped from a balloon over 31 kilometres up and fell for over five minutes before he opened his parachute.

Most jumps in a day

In 1979, an Englishman, David Parchment, made 233 parachute jumps in one day. It took 18 hours, 7 minutes.

First through the sound barrier

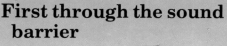

Sound travels at 1,224 kilometres per hour. In 1947, Captain 'Chuck' Yeager was the first man to fly faster than sound in a rocket plane.

Powered by the Sun

Most aeroplane engines burn fuel. This plane has solar panels on the wings which turn sunlight into electricity to work the propeller.

Biggest plane in the world

This giant Hercules flying boat was designed and flown by a rich American, Howard Hughes, in 1947. It has never flown again.

It has eight engines and the largest wing span of any plane ever built – 97.54 metres. Made of wood, it was nicknamed 'Spruce Goose'.

In the First World War (1914-1918) pilots wore leather coats, helmets and goggles to protect them and keep them warm in open cockpits.

In the Second World War (1939-1945) pilots wore helmets with headphones, and an oxygen mask with a microphone to talk to base.

Today a fighter pilot wears a special helmet, like an astronaut's. It protects him when he is flying very high and very fast.

First published in 1981 by Usborne Publishing Ltd, 83-85 Saffron Hill, London, EC1N 8RT, England. Copyright © 1992, 1988 Usborne Publishing Ltd

This edition published in 1997 by Tiger Books International PLC, Twickenham ISBN 1-85501-970-1

Printed in Hong Kong